Global Issues

Climate Change

Cheryl Jakab

Smart Apple Media

This edition first published in 2008 in the United States of America by Smart Apple Media.

Smart Apple Media
2140 Howard Drive West
North Mankato, Minnesota 56003

First published in 2007 by
MACMILLAN EDUCATION AUSTRALIA PTY LTD
627 Chapel Street, South Yarra, Australia 3141

Visit our Web site at www.macmillan.com.au or go directly to www.macmillanlibrary.com.au

Associated companies and representatives throughout the world.

Library of Congress Cataloging-in-Publication Data

Jakab, Cheryl.
    Climate change / by Cheryl Jakab.
    p. cm. — (Global issues)
    Includes index.
    ISBN 978-1-59920-123-8
1. Climatic changes. 2. Climatic changes—Environmental aspects. I. Title.

    QC981.8.C5J35 2007
    551.6—dc22

                                                            2007004556

Edited by Anna Fern
Text and cover design by Cristina Neri, Canary Graphic Design
Page layout by Domenic Lauricella and Cristina Neri
Photo research by Legend Images
Illustrations by Andrew Louey; graphs by Raul Diche
Maps courtesy of Geo Atlas

Printed in U.S.

Acknowledgements
The author and the publisher are grateful to the following for permission to reproduce copyright material:

Front cover inset photograph: Wildflowers near the Tatshenshini River, Alaska, © Photos.com. Earth photograph courtesy of Photodisc.

Background photograph of Earth and magnifying glass image both courtesy of Photodisc.

© Wayne Lawler/AUSCAPE, pp. 7 (bottom), 16; BigStockPhoto, p. 5; © Brownm39/Dreamstime.com, p. 27; © Terrasprite/ Dreamstime.com, p. 24; Jeffrey Dukes, p. 19; Fairfaxphotos, data Bureau of Meteorology, p. 17; © Brian Nolan/Fotolia, pp. 7 (top), 21; Friends of the Helmeted Honeyeater, photo by Margot Craddock, p. 29; China Photos/Getty Images, p. 26; Dimas Ardian/ Getty Images, pp. 7 (right), 25; © brue/iStockphoto.com, pp. 6 (left), 12; © buzbuzzer/iStockphoto.com, p. 22; © fusionphoto/ iStockphoto.com, p. 15; Legendimages, p. 28 ; NASA/Goddard Space Flight Center Scientific Visualization Studio, pp. 8, 9; NASA/MODIS Land Response Team, Aqua Satellite/Jacques Descloitres, p. 20 ; Photolibrary/Science Photolibrary, pp. 6 (bottom), 10; Photos.com, p. 18; Wikimedia Commons, p. 23.

Please note
At the time of printing, the Internet addresses appearing in this book were correct. Owing to the dynamic nature of the Internet, however, we cannot guarantee that all these addresses will remain correct.

Contents

Glossary words
When a word is printed in **bold**, you can look up its meaning in the glossary on page 31.

Facing global issues

Hi there! This is Earth speaking. Will you take a moment to listen to me? I have some very important things to discuss.

We must face up to some urgent environmental problems! All living things depend on my environment, but the way you humans are living at the moment, I will not be able to keep looking after you.

The issues I am worried about are:
- the huge number of people on Earth
- the supply of clean air and water
- wasting resources
- energy supplies for the future
- protecting all living things
- **global warming** and **climate change**

My global challenge to you is to find a **sustainable** way of living. Read on to find out what people around the world are doing to try to help.

Fast fact

In 2005, the **United Nations Environment Program Report**, written by experts from 95 countries, concluded that 60 percent of Earth's resources are being **degraded** or used unsustainably.

What's the issue?
Climate change

The climate of the world is changing. It is happening at a very fast rate, leading to rapid changes in every environment.

Across the world, climates are getting warmer than they were in the recent past. Over the last 100 years, temperatures recorded worldwide are higher on average by about 1.8° F (1°C). This global warming is enough to cause huge changes in weather conditions, storm patterns, winds, and the growth of plants.

What causes global warming?

Many human activities are causing global warming. The main cause is the burning of the **fossil fuels** coal and oil. Burning fossil fuels gives off gases including **carbon dioxide**, which trap the heat of the sun in Earth's **atmosphere**. These **greenhouse gases** cause Earth to heat up.

Fast fact
Twenty thousand years ago, during the last great ice age, the average surface temperature on Earth was about 46° F (8°C). Today, the average surface temperature is about 59° F (15°C).

More storms and hurricanes are being experienced due to global warming.

The most urgent climate change issues around the world include:

- the melting of ice cover at the **poles** and in **glaciers** (see issue 1)
- rising sea levels flooding the land (see issue 2)
- temperatures getting hotter each year (see issue 3)
- more storms and hurricanes (see issue 4)
- human activities continuing to add to global warming (see issue 5)

ARCTIC OCEAN

Arctic Circle

NORTH AMERICA

NORTH PACIFIC OCEAN

Tropic of Cancer

Florida

NORTH ATLANT OCEAN

SOUTH AMERICA

AT

Tropic of Capricorn

ISSUE 4

Florida
More frequent and severe hurricanes. See pages 20–23.

ISSUE 1

Antarctic
The ice cap is melting and getting smaller. See pages 8–11.

around the globe

Fast fact
Earth's climate has had many natural changes, including ice ages, due to changes in average temperature of up to 9°F (5°C).

ISSUE 2

Pacific Islands
Rising sea levels covering low-lying land. See pages 12–15.

ISSUE 5

Indonesia
Burning forests add to greenhouse gases. See pages 24–27.

A S I A

A F R I C A

Equa

Indonesia

Pacific Islands

Tropic of Capric

UTH

NTIC

EAN

A U S T R A L I A

ISSUE 3

Australia
Summer temperatures are the hottest on record. See pages 16–19.

A N T A R C T I C A

Melting ice

Ice fields all over Earth are melting much faster than they are forming. This retreat of ice was the first real evidence of global warming. It is what first alerted scientists to the serious environmental problems associated with climate change.

Earth's ice

Today, **permanent ice** covers almost 10 percent of the land area on Earth. Ice occurs in glaciers, on snow-capped mountains, and in sheets of thick ice across the Antarctic and Arctic.

Since scientists started mapping the ice cover using satellite imaging, they have found that, everywhere, the ice cover is shrinking.

The effects of melting ice

Polar ice reflects heat and light from the sun back into space, and helps keep the planet cool. With the disappearance of ice, Earth's climate could warm up even more. It has been predicted that melting ice could lead to a rise in sea levels of 16 to 20 feet (5–6 m).

Marine mammals, seabirds, and other creatures that depend on food found at the ice edge are already suffering as a result of the global ice melt.

Fast fact
Arctic sea ice decreased by 6 percent between 1978 and 1996.

The Larsen B ice shelf, Antarctica, on January 31, 2002, before it shattered.

CASE STUDY
Antarctic ice melt

Since the 1970s, the ice sheets surrounding Antarctica have been retreating or reducing in size. One example is the Larsen B ice shelf, which today is around half the size it was early in the 1900s.

Ice in the Antarctic

Antarctica is a huge continent permanently covered in ice which has built up over thousands of years. The ice is more than 13,000 feet (4,000 m) thick in places. The great weight of this ice pushes down, pressing some of the ice out at the edges of the continent in glaciers. This forms **icebergs** and **ice floes** that are found around the edge of Antarctica.

The Larsen B ice shelf

The Larsen B ice shelf is a floating shelf about 720 feet (220 m) thick. In January and February 2002, the Larsen B ice shelf shattered and separated from the Antarctic continent. The collapse formed thousands of icebergs in the Weddell Sea. In this one event, about 650 tons of ice broke off the shelf.

Fast fact
Ninety percent of Earth's permanent ice cover is held in the Antarctic ice cap.

The Larsen B ice shelf on March 21, 2002, after it shattered.

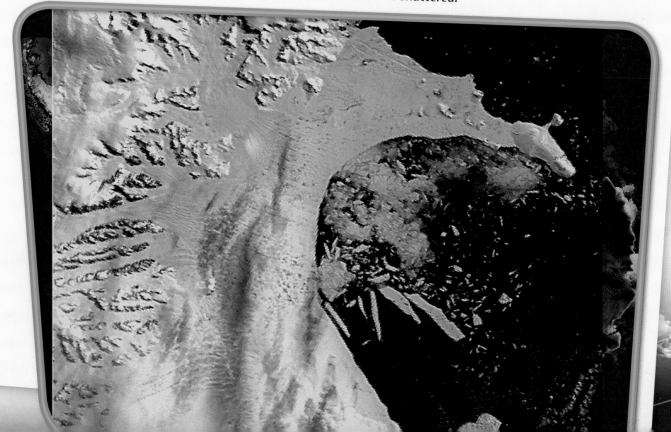

Toward a sustainable future: Collecting evidence of climate change

Gathering evidence of climate change from changes to the ice cover is an important step to understanding the extent of the climate problems we face.

Recording the changes

Today, loss of ice from the Antarctic and Arctic is constantly being observed. Satellite images clearly show the rate at which the ice is retreating. In 2006, glaciers in Greenland were reaching the sea at twice the previous rate, and releasing three to four times more water than they did in the recent past.

Predicting the future

Recording climate change helps us predict and plan for changes that may occur in the future. Many computer models of global climate have been developed based on what has been observed to try to predict the future. In this way, we can plan and prepare for climate change.

Fast fact
Solid particles of air pollution do not add to global warming. They actually reflect light back into space and decrease heating from the sun.

Large pieces of ice break off glaciers as they push out into the sea, forming icebergs.

CASE STUDY:
The greenhouse effect

The climate across the globe is warming due to an increase in greenhouse gases in the atmosphere. Scientists now know that human activity is the biggest cause of the observed changes in climate seen over the past few decades. A buildup of gases from burning fossil fuels has changed Earth's atmosphere, creating an increased **greenhouse effect**.

Natural greenhouse effect

Earth is kept warm by a natural greenhouse effect. Carbon dioxide and other gases trap heat in the atmosphere, just as the walls of a greenhouse trap heat. This is known as the greenhouse effect.

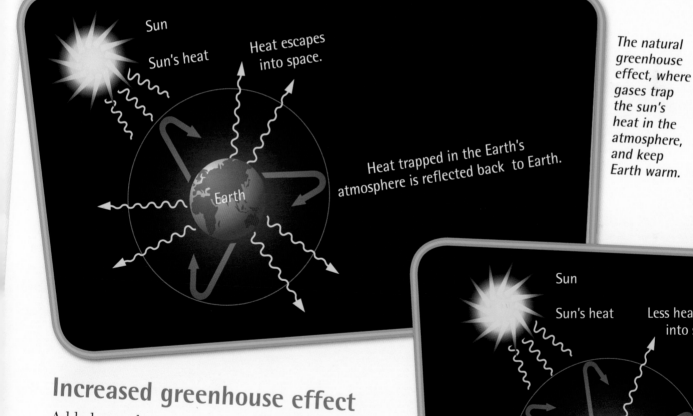

Sun

Sun's heat

Heat escapes into space.

Heat trapped in the Earth's atmosphere is reflected back to Earth.

Earth

The natural greenhouse effect, where gases trap the sun's heat in the atmosphere, and keep Earth warm.

Increased greenhouse effect

Added greenhouse gases in the atmosphere are increasing the greenhouse effect. When fossil fuels are burned, the amount of carbon dioxide in the atmosphere increases. This increased carbon dioxide is trapping more of the sun's heat in the atmosphere, increasing the greenhouse effect and leading to global warming.

The increased greenhouse effect, causing global warming and climate change.

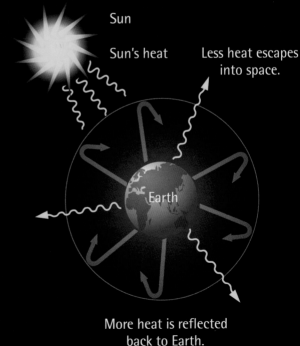

Sun

Sun's heat

Less heat escapes into space.

Earth

More heat is reflected back to Earth.

11

Rising sea levels

Global warming is leading to rising sea levels. As temperatures rise and ice sheets melt, sea levels around the globe rise.

How sea levels rise

The ice cover at the poles holds huge amounts of water. As this water is released from the ice sheets, the level of the oceans must rise. The amount of the rise will depend on how much temperatures rise. The higher the average temperature, the more ice will melt. How much the ice sheets decrease will be matched by the rise in sea level.

What is being lost?

People living in the Arctic and any low-lying islands throughout the world will face losing their homes. As sea levels rise, low-lying land will be flooded. For instance, about 80 percent of the Maldives is less than 3 feet (1 m) above sea level, making rising sea levels a great concern for people living there.

Fast fact
Flooding from rising sea levels will force many millions of people to migrate from low-lying areas such as Tuvalu, the Maldives, and Bangladesh.

Low-lying areas on this island in the Maldives are being flooded by rising sea levels.

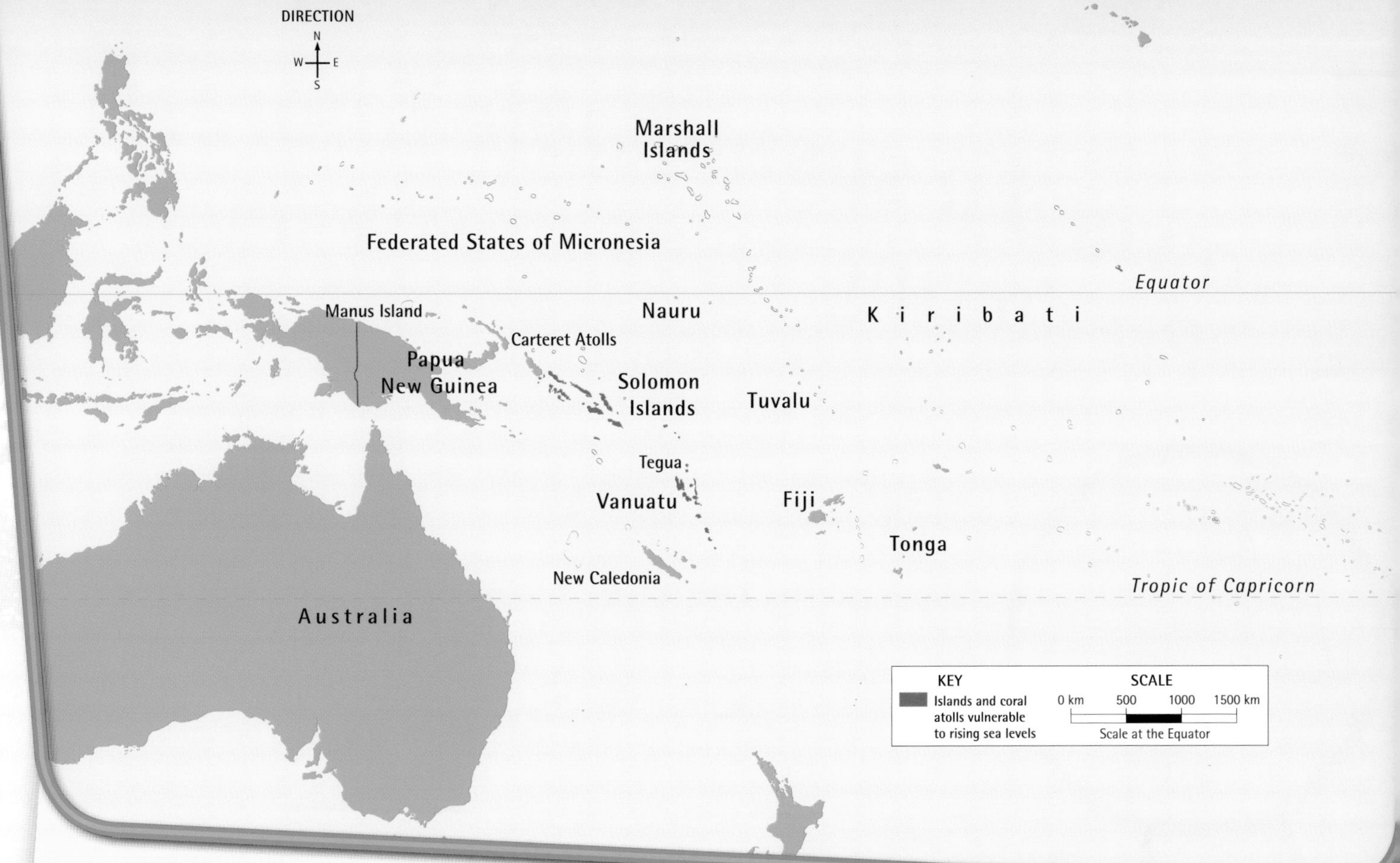
DIRECTION
N
W
E
S
Marshall Islands
Federated States of Micronesia
Manus Island
Nauru
Kiribati
Equator
Carteret Atolls
Papua New Guinea
Solomon Islands
Tuvalu
Tegua
Vanuatu
Fiji
Tonga
New Caledonia
Tropic of Capricorn
Australia
KEY
Islands and coral atolls vulnerable to rising sea levels
SCALE
0 km
500
1000
1500 km
Scale at the Equator

The Pacific Islands shown in red are vulnerable to rising sea levels.

ISSUE 2

CASE STUDY

Pacific Islands

Pacific Islanders living on low-lying **coral atolls** are among the first to be seriously affected by rising sea levels. The people living on these islands are to be the first of many global warming refugees.

Carteret Islands

About 2,000 people from the Carteret Islands in Papua New Guinea are being moved to Bougainville due to rising sea levels. Their low-lying islands are disappearing under the rising seas.

Fast fact
Two uninhabited islands of Kiribati disappeared under rising seas in 1999.

Tegua

Tegua is an island in Vanuatu where, in recent years, the coastline has moved up the shore by 33 to 66 feet (10–20 m). Tegua is one of the few islands in the area that has any high ground. It has a mountain rising more than 985 feet (300 m) above sea level. Tegua is home to just over 60 people who have had to move up their mountain as sea levels rise. As the island now lacks **fresh water**, a relocation program was started in 2002.

Toward a sustainable future: Predicting rises in sea level

Predictions of how much the sea level will rise with global warming vary greatly. It is true that every coastline on every piece of land will be affected by rising sea levels.

Measuring the rise

A network of gauges has been set up to measure long-term global changes in sea level. Knowing the rate of rise will help in planning for the change. The Global Sea Level Observing System provides accurate information on sea levels.

Preparing for the change

Having a good idea of how much sea levels will rise allows people to plan for the future. Some people may decide to prepare for flooding by moving to higher ground. Others may decide to put structures in place, such as sea walls and vegetation, to protect their land from the sea.

Sea levels around Europe are predicted to rise and flood some areas.

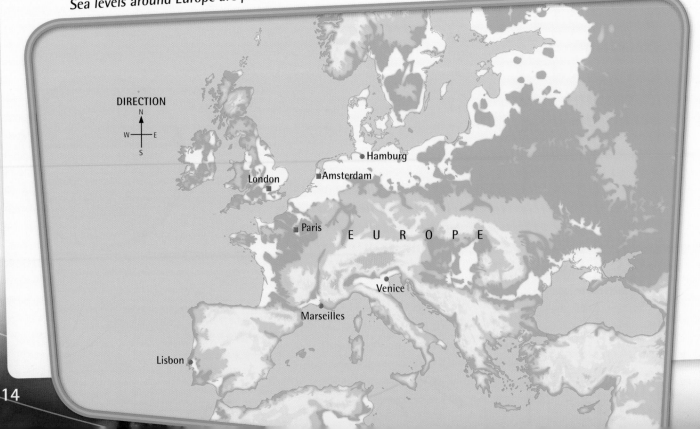

Flooding from rising sea levels will force many people living on river deltas, such as the Mekong in Vietnam, to move.

CASE STUDY
Measures against floods

River deltas are areas of land formed where fast-flowing rivers meet the sea. They form rich **habitat** for living things, including people, but they also have problems with flooding. Preparations need to be made to prevent millions of people living on river deltas from being displaced by rising waters.

Using flood retarding basins

In the past, large levee banks were built close to the river to prevent flooding disasters on deltas. The flood plains behind the levees could then have houses built on them.

It is now believed that building banks near the river will not be effective against increased flooding. Instead, the flood banks need to be built further back from the river. Building flood banks further from the river creates a wide area of flood plain called a "retarding basin." These large areas cannot be built on, but can be useful green spaces in crowded cities.

Fast fact
Six major river deltas that hold very large populations are:
- Bengal Delta, Bangladesh
- Mekong Delta, Vietnam
- Nile Delta, Egypt
- Yantze Delta, China
- Mississippi Delta, U.S.
- Godavaru Delta, India

15

Record temperatures

In 2005, the highest temperatures on record were experienced across the globe. Temperatures today are the highest seen for at least 1,000 years. Rainfall in many areas is also decreasing. As temperatures rise, areas that are already hot and dry become even harsher.

Increasing world temperatures

In the 1900s, worldwide temperatures rose by at least 0.9 to 1.8°F (0.5–1°C). In the early 2000s, temperatures continued to rise. Experts agree that the record high temperatures are evidence of global warming.

Effects of global warming

The 30 percent increase in carbon dioxide in the last 100 years has caused an overall temperature increase. This global warming is also causing:

- changes in rainfall patterns and storm activity
- changes in ocean currents and winds
- changes in plant growth and flowering, and in animal behaviors

Scientists are still working out how these changes are affecting the health of the planet.

Fast fact
In 2005, worldwide temperatures were on average about 0.9°F (0.5°C) higher than they were in the past 30 years.

Many areas are experiencing lower rainfall and higher temperatures than normal, leaving animals without enough food to eat.

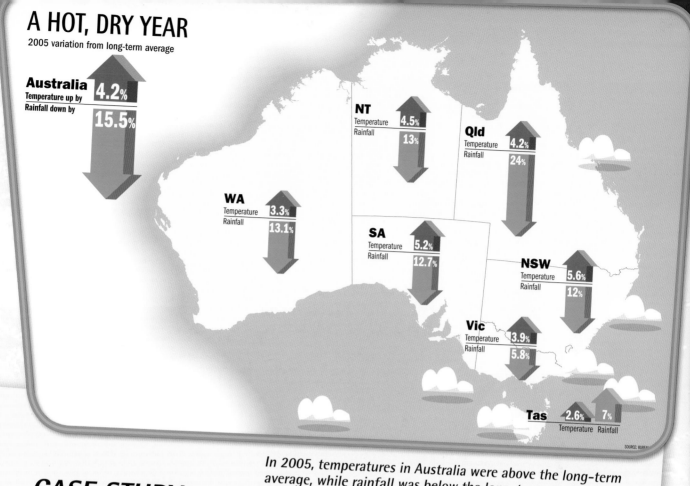

A HOT, DRY YEAR

2005 variation from long-term average

Australia
Temperature up by **4.2%**
Rainfall down by **15.5%**

NT
Temperature **4.5%**
Rainfall **13%**

Qld
Temperature **4.2%**
Rainfall **24%**

WA
Temperature **3.3%**
Rainfall **13.1%**

SA
Temperature **5.2%**
Rainfall **12.7%**

NSW
Temperature **5.6%**
Rainfall **12%**

Vic
Temperature **3.9%**
Rainfall **5.8%**

Tas **2.6%** **7%**
Temperature Rainfall

SOURCE: BUREAU

In 2005, temperatures in Australia were above the long-term average, while rainfall was below the long-term average.

CASE STUDY

Australia in 2005

In 2005, most of Australia experienced higher than average temperatures. In fact, it was the hottest year on record.

Highest temperatures recorded

Temperatures recorded throughout Australia in 2005 were the hottest since records began. The average temperature was 1.8°F (1°C) above the average recorded between 1961 and 1999.

Much of the area of Australia is **desert** and poor farming land. As temperatures rise and the land becomes drier, farming and living will become more difficult.

Predicted temperatures

Melbourne, Victoria, currently has an average top temperature of around 68°F (20°C). It is predicted that by 2030 this could rise to an average of 72°F (22°C), and, by 2070, about 77°F (25°C). It is also predicted that rainfall will decrease.

Toward a sustainable future: Living with climate change

Changing climate conditions cannot be ignored. As the temperature gets hotter, rainfall changes, and carbon dioxide levels rise, people will need to change what they do to survive in the new environmental conditions. They will need to learn about what crops to grow for food, and how crops and animals will respond to the new conditions.

Fast fact

The Intergovernmental Panel on Climate Change predicts that average world temperatures may rise by as much as 9° F (5° C) by 2100.

Different growth patterns in plants

Due to global warming, plants are growing differently. For instance, in many areas, plants are blooming earlier in the season. This will affect the animals that live on these plants, as well as the harvesting of crops and the types of crops that are planted.

Adapting to changes

As global climate changes, people will need to change the way they use their resources. They must plan for different seasons from those experienced in the past. We must accept that global warming will change our environment for a long time to come.

Many plants, such as these wildflowers in Alaska, are blooming earlier than usual.

Jasper Ridge Biological Reserve was the subject of a study on the impact of climate change.

CASE STUDY

Jasper Ridge Global Change Project

The Jasper Ridge Global Change Project was designed to study the impact of future global environmental changes. Between 1998 and 2001, researchers from Stanford University, in the United States, studied plants in 160 plots of land at Jasper Ridge Biological Preserve.

The experiment

The experiment was set up to mirror four conditions that climate experts predict could exist 100 years from now:

- a temperature increase of 1.8°F (1°C)
- a 50 percent rise in rainfall
- double the amount of carbon dioxide in the air
- higher concentrations of pollution in the soil

Study results

The study results showed growth of the plants in the area was different in each of the conditions. A surprise result was that all plants grew poorly in the high concentrations of carbon dioxide tested. Many people had predicted that plants would grow better in high carbon dioxide conditions.

The study results will help scientists find plant strains that can cope with the expected climate changes.

Fast fact
Wildflowers in the test plots grew less well and may in fact become endangered by the predicted conditions.

More hurricanes

One big climate change seen early in the 1990s and 2000s was an increase in extreme weather. There have been more high-intensity hurricanes across the world in recent years. It is predicted the frequency of hurricanes and other extreme weather events will continue to rise with global warming.

What is a hurricane?

Hurricanes are violent wind storms that begin near the Equator, particularly in the West Indies, Caribbean Sea, and Gulf of Mexico. Hurricanes in the western Pacific are known as typhoons. Hurricanes form when high sea temperatures combine with high amounts of moisture in the air and wind.

Hurricane categories

The hurricane intensity category system developed in the 1970s calculates the destructive force of hurricanes. Increase in sea surface temperatures leads to more category 5 hurricanes.

Hurricane Dennis, off the coast of Florida.

Hurricane category	Description	Wind speed (miles per hour)	Damage
1	Weak	74–95	Minimal damage to plants
2	Moderate	96–110	Moderate damage to houses
3	Strong	111–130	Extensive damage to structures
4	Very strong	131–155	Extreme damage
5	Devastating	Greater than 155	Catastrophic damage

These homes in New Orleans collapsed during flooding from the storm surge caused by the high winds of Hurricane Katrina.

CASE STUDY
Florida hurricanes

Hurricane Katrina, which hit New Orleans in 2005, was a category 5 hurricane. Hurricane Katrina displaced more than half a million people.

Damage in New Orleans

New Orleans lies on the delta formed by the Mississippi River as it enters the sea. Hurricanes hitting deltas produce storm damage, as well as extreme flooding due to storm surges that come with the hurricane. Deltas are naturally vulnerable to flooding because they are low-lying. In the case of Hurricane Katrina, not only was the storm damage huge, but the storm surge flooding had devastating effects.

Fast fact

It is estimated that by 2050 about 20 percent of the area around the Mississippi Delta will be flooded.

Toward a sustainable future: Combating global warming

Global warming is a worldwide problem that will only be combated by worldwide solutions. Climate changes, such as increased hurricane activity and increases in temperature, are happening worldwide.

The international community needs to accept that climate change is real and an extremely urgent environmental issue. There is now general agreement that the increased greenhouse effect is contributing to increased temperatures.

Carbon dioxide emissions are still rising.

Framework Convention on Climate Change

The first step in international cooperation in combating climate change came in 1992. At a United Nations meeting, the Framework Convention on Climate Change set targets for industrialized nations for carbon dioxide **emissions**. The target was that emissions be no higher in 2000 than they were in 1990. These targets were not achieved.

Even if carbon dioxide emissions could be stopped suddenly today, extreme weather due to global warming, such as hurricanes, would continue for many years. Global warming will be hard to reverse and combating it is a long-term project.

Fast fact
"I say the debate is over. We know the science, and we see the threat. The time for action is now."

Arnold Schwarzenegger, actor and Governor of California, January 2006

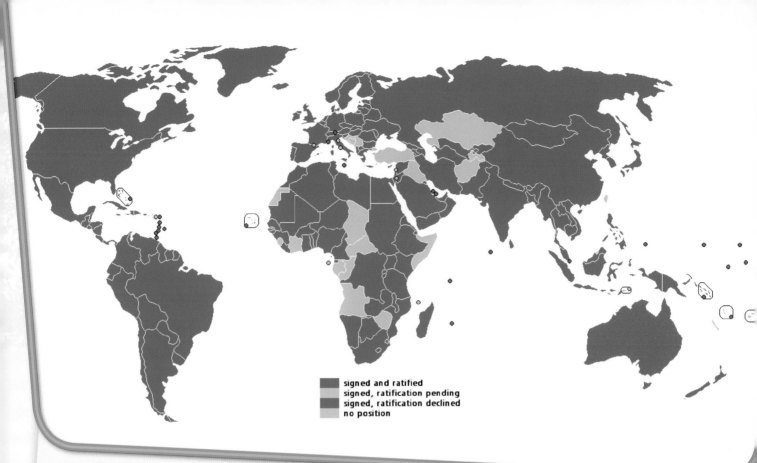

signed and ratified
signed, ratification pending
signed, ratification declined
no position

This map shows the participation of all countries in the Kyoto Protocol.

CASE STUDY

Kyoto Protocol targets

The 1997 Kyoto Protocol is an international treaty on climate change developed to help put in place the United Nations Framework Convention on Climate Change.

The Kyoto Protocol sets targets for reducing carbon dioxide emissions. Overall, the targets set greenhouse gas emissions to fall to 30 to 50 percent below the 1990 level by 2050.

Positive actions

Industrialized countries signing the Kyoto Protocol agreed:
- to reduce their greenhouse gas emissions by 25 to 30 percent between 1990 and 2020
- to reduce their greenhouse emissions by 85 to 90 percent between 1990 and 2050.

The U.S. and Australia were not among the 141 countries to agree to make the targets legally binding. However, a number of states in the U.S. have pledged to adopt Kyoto-style limits and Australia is pursuing its own agreements in the local Asian region.

Fast fact
During the past 20 years, about three-quarters of human-made carbon dioxide emissions were from burning fossil fuels.

ISSUE 4

23

Increase in greenhouse gases

Greenhouse gases in the atmosphere are still increasing due to burning fossil fuels and land clearing. Although international agreements are in place, changes in behaviors are happening very slowly.

Greenhouse gases

Many human activities are still releasing huge amounts of greenhouse gases. Carbon dioxide, **methane**, and other greenhouse gases are being added to the atmosphere at an alarming rate. Even with huge reductions in emissions, reversal of climate change will be slow. It will take a long time to return levels of greenhouse gas in the atmosphere back to preindustrial levels.

Plants and greenhouse gases

Plants help keep down levels of the major greenhouse gas, carbon dioxide. Plants take in carbon dioxide and release oxygen as they grow, so growing plants reduces carbon dioxide in the air. Cutting down forests and other plant communities is continuing to reduce the number of plants available that could be helping lower greenhouse gases in the air.

Fast fact
Today, rain forests cover less than 8 percent of Earth's surface, which is less than half of the area the rain forests covered when modern clearing began.

Forest clearing adds to the rise in greenhouse gases.

Haze from wildfires, lit by farmers to clear land, blankets Pekanbaru Airport on the Indonesian island of Sumatra, 2005.

CASE STUDY

Indonesian forests burning

Indonesia has the world's largest reserves of **tropical forest** outside the Amazon. Logging has been intensive in some areas, but forests still cover about two-thirds of the total land area. Each year, huge clouds of smoke billow up from burning forests in Indonesia.

Slash and burn

Slashing down and burning large areas of forest is a common method of clearing forest for farms. This technique causes an enormous amount of environmental damage, including the release of carbon dioxide into the atmosphere. Burning forests increases greenhouse gases and global warming, destroys habitat, and increases erosion.

Rapid destruction

At the current rate of destruction, lowland rain forests in Indonesia and across the globe will disappear in 20 years. Indonesia and Brazil account for 45 percent of the total loss of tropical rain forest worldwide. Annual rates of **deforestation** in 52 tropical countries nearly doubled from 1981 to 1990.

Fast fact
Worldwide, there is 20 percent to 33 percent less tropical rain forest today than existed in the past.

Toward a sustainable future: Decreasing greenhouse gases

Decreasing levels of carbon dioxide and other greenhouse gases in the atmosphere is the best way to combat global warming. International agreements designed to combat global warming center on decreasing the emissions of carbon dioxide, methane, and other greenhouse gases, and increasing forest cover on Earth.

Decreasing emissions

Any reduction in greenhouse gas emissions will reduce the greenhouse effect being experienced across the globe. Many communities, businesses, and nations are working on ways to reduce greenhouse gas emissions in an effort to combat climate change. However, many people, companies, and nations are unwilling to change their behaviors.

Increasing plant cover

Fast fact
Trees planted between 2001 and 2005 increased the forest cover in China by 2 percent.

Worldwide efforts to save existing forests and plant more trees are helping to fight global warming. Deforestation has added to global warming, and must be halted and reversed. Increasing the land covered by forests, **mangroves**, and other plant communities is an important strategy in reducing carbon dioxide levels.

A Chinese girl waters a tree she has planted near her home on National Tree-Planting Day, 2006.

CASE STUDY
Borneo's forests

The Southeast Asian island of Borneo is home to many **species** of plants and animals found nowhere else. It is also home to some of the world's oldest rain forest. Today's use of the forest is unsustainable. The forest in Borneo is rapidly declining due to land clearing by slash and burn farming and logging.

Preventing the forests of Borneo being cleared and burned would:

- reduce greenhouse gas in the air
- protect plants and animal species
- provide a more sustainable way of life for the people

Forest use in the future

A more sustainable future would be to develop the forests as wildlife reserves that could attract tourists. Protecting endangered species by protecting the forests provides a more sustainable way of life for the people at the same time as helping combat global warming.

Fast fact
About 18 percent of species in Borneo are **threatened** and 3.2 percent are endangered, including at least 78 plant species that grow nowhere else.

This orangutan's home in the forest of Borneo is among the fastest disappearing habitats in the world.

Borneo's plant and animal species

Plants	Animals
rhododendron	
orchid	elephants, rhinoceroses, and wild ox
pitcher plant	orangutan, gibbon, proboscis monkey, and macaque monkey
fruit trees including coconut palm, orange, banana, and mango	tiger cat, tapir, honey bear, and porcupine
timber trees including teak, ironwood, ebony, and sandalwood.	flying squirrel and flying fox
	reptiles including crocodile, lizards, python, and other snakes
	birds including eagles, falcons, vultures, parrots, peacocks, flamingos, hornbills, pheasant, swift, and woodpecker.

What can you do?
Cut greenhouse emissions

You may think that just one person cannot do much, but everyone can help. If every person is careful, the little differences can add up.

Individual actions

Each time you travel in the car, switch on a light, or cook food, chances are the energy used has come from burning fossil fuels. Every time you use energy from burning fossil fuels, more greenhouse gas is released, adding to global warming.

The solution to global warming is long-term and depends on all people cooperating. Government programs cannot achieve anything without the support of the people. Everyone needs to take individual action to help reduce greenhouse gas emissions as well as expect governments to regulate greenhouse gas emissions.

Reduce greenhouse emissions

You can make a difference to carbon dioxide emissions by:
- being aware of wasting energy
- saving electricity by switching off lights when you leave a room
- not leaving the television, computers, or other electrical appliances in standby mode

Switch off the power to electrical appliances rather than leaving them in standby mode.

These school children are planting trees in a nature reserve to create habitat for opossums, birds, and other fauna.

Grow some plants

Planting trees or creating a garden helps improve air quality, reduces greenhouse gases and other pollutants in the air, and makes the environment more pleasant.

What to do

Find an area that needs some plants where you could carry out a revegetation or garden project. It might be part of a school ground, a park, or your own home. Design a garden that you and your friends could create. Think about the type of plants that may be the best for the area.

- Do you want or need large trees, small ground-covering plants, vegetables or fruit trees, or flowers?
- Are there local or native plants that you could grow?
- Think about how you could raise funds to make the garden.

You do not need to buy plants. You can grow them from cuttings or seeds collected from plants in the area.

Toward a sustainable future

Well, I hope you now see that if you accept my challenge your world will be a better place. There are many ways to work toward a sustainable future. Imagine it . . . a world with:

- a stable climate
- clean air and water
- nonpolluting, **renewable** fuel supplies
- plenty of food
- resources for everyone
- healthy natural environments

This is what you can achieve if you work together with my natural systems.

We must work together to live sustainably. That will mean a better environment and a better life for all living things on Earth, now and in the future.

Web sites

For further information on climate change, visit these Web sites:

- United Nations Framework Convention on Climate Change
  http://unfccc.int/essential_background/items/2877.php
- United States Environmental Protection Agency www.epa.gov/globalwarming
- NASA climate change research http://gcmd.nasa.gov
- Woods Hole Research Centre www.whrc.org/globalwarming/

Glossary

atmosphere
the layer of gases surrounding Earth

carbon dioxide
a colorless, odorless gas in the atmosphere

climate change
changes to the usual weather patterns in an area

coral atolls
coral islands, consisting of a horseshoe-shaped reef enclosing a shallow lagoon

deforestation
removal or clearing of forest cover

degraded
run down or reduced to a lower quality

desert
area of low plant cover and low rainfall

emissions
substances released into the environment

fossil fuels
fuels such as oil, coal, and gas, which formed underground from the remains of animals and plants that lived millions of years ago

fresh water
water low enough in salt and other chemicals to be suitable for drinking

glaciers
rivers of moving ice

global warming
an increase in the average temperature on Earth

greenhouse effect
warming of Earth due to heat being trapped by the atmosphere

greenhouse gases
gases that help trap the sun's heat in the atmosphere

habitat
the area used by a living thing to provide its needs

ice age
period when temperatures were lower and large areas of Earth were covered with ice

icebergs
large pieces of ice floating on sea which have broken off a glacier or ice sheet

ice cap
ice-covered areas at the North and South poles

ice floes
sheets of moving ice that have broken from a large glacier or ice shelf

mangroves
forests in the intertidal area of coastlines

methane
a gas that is given off from burning fossil fuels and decomposing vegetation (including the digestion of plants by animals)

permanent ice
ice in glaciers and ice sheets that does not melt

polar ice
ice near the poles of Earth

poles
areas of Earth at the extreme north and south, which are always cold

renewable
a resource that can be constantly supplied and which does not run out

species
living things of the same grouping

sustainable
a way of living that does not use up natural resources

threatened
species under threat of extinction

tropical forest
areas of forest with high temperatures and high rainfall that are found near the Equator

United Nations Environment Program
a program, which is part of the United Nations, set up to encourage nations to care for the environment

Index